Playing Pirates:

The Construction of Shared Fantasy and Identity Performance in the Renaissance Festival Subculture

Heather E. Dumas

Playing Pirates: The Construction of Shared Fantasy and Identity
Performance in the Renaissance Festival Subculture
Copyright ©2013 by Heather Ember Amsden Dumas

Woolmonger Publishing
evergreenwitches@gmail.com
ISBN 9798334316560

Dedication

This is dedicated to those rennies who took me in, treated me as part of the crew, and willingly played along with my game as I played along with theirs.
Huzzah!

Table of Contents

Abstract

This book examines how the renaissance festival setting offers a context for non normative identity performance within a carnivalesque setting in which the construction of shared fantasy is the basis of social processes. It also asks how social forces, such as popular media's romanticized version of history, may influence participants' identity expression and interactions in the subculture as a setting in which they can find meaningful interaction with others who share their social paradigm. Relevant findings can help us better understand identity performance, as well as how culture is constructed through interactions based on shared fantasy. Findings and theoretical applications may also apply to similar social venues including science fiction fandom and conventions, massively-multiplayer online role playing games (MMORPGs), live action role playing (LARP), historical reenactment societies, and even other festival settings in which an alternate, non-normative identity is expressed. The participatory element of this activity, where interaction takes place face to face in an immersive setting which is set apart from the outside world, makes renaissance festivals of particular interest to sociological study.

Introduction

Approaching the gates of the renaissance festival, one walks along a forest path to where ticket booths flank a gap in the tall board fence. Young women and men in medieval clothing process payments and hand over tickets. Once inside the first fence, other patrons in plain clothes and dozens of people dressed in all manner of renaissance costumes mingle happily, many greeting one another like old friends. Then a voice calls for silence and the King steps out onto the roof of the tall stone tower to one side of a huge rough-hewn wooden gate like that of a fort or town. There is a brief introduction of some of the nobility and a pair of knights mounted on horseback. Then the King calls for the gates to be opened, and the crowd cheers. Walking past the ticket counters and inside the open gate, one is immediately aware that this is another reality. A band of musicians with fiddles, guitars, and other instruments play while a troupe of faeries dance and giggle, stopping to hug people they seem to know as they walk past. A crew of pirates rushes the gate and into the village, apparently more bent on merriment than actual pillaging. And all around, ladies in colorful gowns and men in kilts talk, and laugh, and stroll along the gravel walkways past the shops and craftspeople hawking their wares. This is where the magic happens.

Since the 1960s, renaissance festivals have been on the fringes of American culture. They are, at their most basic level, theme parks. The entire fair grounds are set up to look like a romanticized version of a renaissance village on a festival day. All the workers dress in renaissance costumes and speak with some semblance of the dialect of the times. Every renaissance festival has its own version of the same stock entertainments. There are stage shows, a joust, eateries and pubs, streets full of brightly dressed visitors, and shops where visitors may purchase items which mimic the time period to varying degrees of historical accuracy. The festival atmosphere sets activity there apart from everyday life in the way Bakhtin (1968) describes any carnival as a time and place in which norms are changed, often inverted. And because the real world's social rules don't necessarily apply, the renfaire, as it is called by those who regularly attend, offers a unique opportunity for participants to express aspects of themselves which might otherwise carry a great deal of social stigma—that of the label of "geek" or "nerd"—were these individuals to dress, speak, and behave so outside the faire's gates (extra 'e' intentional, as used within the subculture to mimic old fashioned spelling patterns).

This study examines how the renaissance festival setting offers a context for nonnormative, though not detrimentally deviant, identity performance within a carnivalesque setting in which the construction of shared fantasy is the basis of social processes. It also asks what social forces, including social strain and the influence of popular media's romanticized version of history, may influence participants toward retreatism into the subculture as a social setting in which they can find authentic identity expression and meaningful interactions with others who share their social paradigm.

Renaissance Festivals

"Pre-electric England was a realm lit only by fire, and in the pre-industrial age the smell of smoke and burning wood was common for both peasant and noble" (KorolEvans 2009:85). As one walks through the gates of any renaissance festival, the senses are flooded with colors, sounds, and smells which are not often encountered in twenty-first century America. Corseted ladies in flowing skirts walk alongside Vikings in fur pelts and swashbuckling pirates. A vivid array of colors—on clothing, buildings, and even human hair—is splashed across the scene. Purple is much more prevalent than history would tell, and one is likely to encounter a number of fanciful characters wearing fairy wings or fox tails. Ale flows from multiple pubs, and food ranging from enormous turkey legs to bread bowls full of stew is available at almost every turn. And lining every "street," as the paths through the festival grounds are called, are shops and tents filled with medieval-style merchandise, much of it handcrafted by those who work the booths.

For some patrons the festival is simply a huge outdoor craft show which provides a unique shopping venue. For others the faire means an opportunity to partake of alcohol without the stigma of public drunkenness. To others, this is a place to bring their children for a day of fun. However, a significant number of patrons who pay to enter the gates seem to, at some time throughout their visit, experience what has termed a state of intrasticiancy, a context in which the fantasy reality of the faire overlaps with that of real personal experiences. It is somewhere in which participants can suspend disbelief and temporarily become caught up in the moment, playing along with the fantasy of a timespace existing both at once in the sixteenth and twenty-first centuries (Korol-Evans 2009). Digital cameras and smartphones capture the moment when the kids meet the king. Credit cards purchase mugs of ale and roast turkey legs from costumed tavern wenches. Yet the presence of the current-day items and the patrons in jeans and t-shirts does not serve to detract from the overall feeling of experiencing the faire as a renaissance village on a festival day.

I am concerned here with those persons who work at the festivals, adopt characters or alternate personas within the group, and make lifestyle changes which affect their way of life outside the events themselves. There is a certain striving for the authentic experience, if not historical accuracy although that is a concern for some, which goes on within this subculture. It is this quest for a more meaningful way of living, based in the internal social structure and collective identity of those who consider themselves "rennies," which presents itself for examination. Whether social strain, the influence of popular media, or other basis for personal fantasy, many factors may work to drive participants toward retreatism into this subculture as a social setting in which they can find meaningful interaction with others in this shared fantasy. I do not here consider the "tourists" or patrons who simply attend the occasional renaissance festival or similar event, dressed in everyday clothes and only buying the odd souvenir, as members of the subculture. While there are certainly a large number of them who attend renaissance faires, they are not my concern for this study.

Sociological Relevance

New technologies and means of connecting with persons who share similar interests have made fantasy social contexts an increasingly important area of sociological study. Some fantasy subculture communities exist online through gaming and other platforms. Others might be found using the internet, then meeting in face to face interactive settings, such as science fiction conventions or music festivals, where participants cultivate an alternate expression of identity which is different from that they perform in their daily lives. Renaissance festival participants have their own community centered around this immersive and interactive fantasy, both in and outside the festival setting, but the festival itself provides a social environment which allows for the performance of non-normative identities which might be deemed deviant outside the festival gates. Examination of this subculture may help sociologists to understand how the shared fantasy created by popular media and fandom, along with the collective socialization processes of the participants themselves, can lead to retreat into a shared social fantasy setting and non-normative identity expression therein.

Fantasy subcultures such as that of renaissance festivals can be viewed as a prosocial retreat into subculture that is an innovative adaptation to stigma and general social strain sprung from feelings of outsiderdom or a sense of not fitting in with mainstream society to some degree. Examining the social processes in this context can help us better understand identity performance, as well as how culture is constructed through interactions based on shared fantasy. Findings and theoretical applications may also relate to similar social venues including science fiction fandom and conventions (Lancaster 1999), massively-multiplayer online role playing games (Nardi 2010, Gilsdorf 2009), both live action and tabletop role playing games (McGonigal 2011, Bowman 2010), historical reenactment societies, and even other festival settings such as Burning Man. The participatory element of this activity, where interaction takes place face to face in an immersive setting which is set apart from the outside world makes renaissance festivals of particular interest to sociologists.

Research Questions

This study seeks to answer several questions relevant to existing scholarly literature in the fields of sociology, performance studies, and fandom and leisure. First, how is the shared fantasy of romanticized history constructed at renaissance festivals and in the "rennie" subculture that exists within that context? Fine (1983) addresses the social construction of shared fantasy in role playing games. The similar element of an idealized historical context exists in both settings, as well as by many of the popular cultural influences which may inform participants' performances of self and shared meanings of interactions. Korol-Evans, in her book Renaissance Festivals: Merrying the Past and Present (2009), considers the intrasticive nature of this social setting in which the 21st and 16th centuries exist simultaneously, giving a rich description of both setting and performance with particular attention to the variation in levels of immersion. Themes of play (Huizinga 1950) and social construction (Berger & Luckmann 1966) also inform this study.

Second, how do participants become interested and involved in this subculture? Both Korol-Evans (2009) and Cramer (2010) explore the medieval re-creationist subculture, describing the initiatory process of becoming involved and what factors influence that process. Experts in social deviance, Becker (1963) and Agnew (1997) both offer insight into deviant subculture involvement.

Third, how is identity performed in the renaissance festival setting? What influences the construction of these presumably alternate or non-normative identity performances, and how do they differ from identities performed outside the festival or the subculture? Goffman's classic, The Performance of Self in Everyday Life (1959), is the canonical basis for studies of social and identity performance, and provides a theoretical basis for exploring the variation in frontstage and backstage identities and interactions. However, as appears to be the nature of this subculture, the fantasy element in identity performance (Fine 1983, Korol-Evans 2009, Cramer 2010) leaves many questions concerning how these fantasies are constructed, how they manifest at the renaissance festival, and even why this social environment in particular is so conducive to their expression.

Fourth, to what degree participation in renaissance festivals and affiliation with this subculture affect participants' lives outside of the renaissance faire? Korol-Evans and Cramer discuss the juxtaposition of "real life" to the immersive world of the festival setting. And deviance theorists such as Agnew and Becker provide a framework for examining social strain and outsiderdom, respectively. However, questions remain unanswered as to how participation in the renaissance festival as a social setting affects participants' lives outside the faire and during the off season, aside from the general "nerd" stigma associated with such activities in mainstream society.

Background Research

The roots of this research are anchored in some informal work I did as an undergraduate student for a course in deviant subcultures. Because I have always been interested in the medieval and renaissance eras, and had previously visited festivals in other parts of the country, I rounded up several friends for a trip to a renaissance faire in our region. At the time I departed for the faire that day, I had not yet chosen a topic for my paper for the deviant subcultures class. However, observing the culture of the faire site with a sociological imagination, it did not take long before I was formulating a plan that culminated in a term paper about the renaissance festival subculture, made possible in part by the opportunities afforded and contacts met on that day's outing.

That initial trip afforded me later entre' into the renaissance festivals I visited for this project, and that earlier work led to this more extensive research project. Having done a small amount of research into this subculture, I saw the opportunity to study the social construction of reality, and in particular the relationship between fantasy and identity in a whole new light in this exemplary model of shared fantasy and the widespread non-normative performance of identity that is the basis of interaction within this context.

One individual—playing the part of a pirate—whom I met during that first trip to the renaissance festival as an undergraduate, proved particularly helpful, and has served as one of my guides within the subculture, introducing me around and helping me become acclimated. It was through my connection with him that I was able to later become acquainted with, and somewhat integrated into, an informal group of "pirates" who served as the primary group of playtrons whom I observed, interviewed, and attended faires with throughout the course of my research. It is by this good fortune of being able to build rapport with this group of people that I was able to attain the insider's view into how renfaire playtrons go about creating and performing identity as manifested in their faire personas, as well as forming networks and social bonds that make up their group identity as well. Because this group had chosen to portray themselves as pirates, I joined them in dressing the part and occasionally role playing as a pirate myself when the interaction in a given situation seemed to call for it. The experience lent an authenticity to my observations that I might not

18

otherwise have been privy to, and I am certain that by showing my willingness to participate in their activities gained me enough of their trust to get the in-depth responses I did during interviews and informal conversations.

Concepts and Framing

A Brief History of Renaissance Festivals

The first renaissance festival was started by theatre history instructor Phyllis Patterson in 1962 in southern California, as a fundraiser for a youth drama center. The intent was to create an atmosphere which offered an idealized version of sixteenth century England, without the plagues and poor sanitation. At first it was difficult for Patterson to find craftspeople to populate her festival village; the handcrafts culture of the 1960s, which is still strong within the renaissance festival community today, had not yet begun to take on popularity. Her first shopkeeper was a sandal maker who was soon joined by potters, weavers, and other hobbyists (Korol-Evans 2009).

What grew to become the Southern California Renaissance Pleasure Faire provided an escape from the strains of the outside world, at least for a few hours, not only for paying visitors, but for the actors, craftspeople, and food merchants who worked there. "Even today, spectators often attend festivals to experience a sense of belonging that perhaps they do not have in their lives outside of the faire" (Korol-Evans 2009:21). Patrons can participate in the life of the festival in numerous ways depending on their own level of comfort in this strange setting. The faire embodies what has been described as the essence of carnival, in which everyday norms and identities can be set aside in order to express the outrageous (Bakhtin 1968). It is a matter of personal choice whether each individual acts upon this invitation to do so. And it is the job of the festival personnel to create that carnivalesque atmosphere. "Everyone who came through those 19 gates, at least in some way, needed the same escape we did, and we tried to give it to them" (Korol-Evans 2009:58).

Constructing Shared Fantasy and the Act of Play

The "intrastice" which Korol-Evans (2009) describes is not an entirely new concept to scholars of subculture. Stahl describes a similar social state in "a terrain that is often simultaneously here, there, and everywhere" (1999:27). The intrastice is a constructed temporal-spatial state in which things of two seemingly contradicting social settings are able to exist simultaneously without any offense being taken to the paradoxical idiosyncrasies (Korol-Evans 2009). The interactions between festival participants, or participants and objects or the setting itself, within the intrastice take on the liberties of carnival, but they also acquire meanings specific to the constructed culture of the renaissance festival itself. Participants base the meaning of their interactions at the festival on prior life experiences to frame their faire encounters, therefore each individual experiences the faire differently in the intrastice. "The festival offers opportunities for patrons to enter different levels of intrasticiancy, depending upon their personal needs" (Korol-Evans 2009:59).

The element of play is something that is present in all human societies, set apart from the toil of work and the banality of everyday activity (Huizinga 1950). "The reality of everyday life is overcast by the penumbra of our dreams" (Berger and Luckmann 1966:45). We all take part in recreational activities, be they relaxing such as reading or watching television, or more active in the way of sport or playing music. But it is play, with its participatory and imaginative nature, set apart from other forms of social interaction, which manifests in the construction of shared fantasy cultures and the formation of an often alternative identity expressed within. Huizinga asks the questions, "To what extent does the civilization we live in still develop in play-forms? How far does the play-spirit dominate the lives of those who share that civilization" (1950:195).

Bakhtin (1968) writes that the carnival setting, that of the festival which is set apart in time and place from daily activities, creates a social environment in which the rules are quite different from those of the everyday world. "Custom grants the right of a certain freedom and familiarity, the right to break the usual norms of social relations" (Bakhtin 1968:200). Certain festivals, events, organizations, and less formal groups create this carnivalesque atmosphere by constructing shared fantasy environments in what Fine calls contemporary urban leisure subcultures (1983). The subject of this study is one such group, the frequent participants of renaissance festival—the performers, craftspeople, and "playtrons", meaning paying patrons who dress in costume and play along—who make up the subculture apart from the more tourist-like patrons who only visit occasionally and wear mainstream clothes when they do.

The renaissance festival exists in the realm of play, not just for young children but for adults too, through which one is transported into this other world with its own culture and set of meanings, either as an audience member or by fanciful interactions with others who are playing along. This playful re-creation of certain aspects of history is what Korol-Evans (2009) calls historical elaboration which elaborates on history through a fantasy culture setting. She distinguishes this from living history or reenactment of specific historical events. She cites Bakhtin in her description of renaissance faires as carnivalesque settings in which participants openly take on personas sometimes very different from their everyday identity by donning costumes and interacting under norms which are distinctly different from those outside the festival.

It is important to understand the nature of cultures based on shared fantasy and their construction in order to better appreciate how and why participants might become involved. It is generally accepted among symbolic interactionists that society and culture are socially constructed, that the interwoven matrix of shared meanings constitutes the way members of a given society perceive the world and how they interact with one another. Berger and Luckmann (1966) wrote of how this intersubjectivity of everyday life is contrasted with the inner workings of an individual's mind in the form of dreams and other imaginative states such as play. "Compared to the reality of everyday life, other realities appear as finite provinces of meaning, enclaves within the paramount reality marked by circumscribed meanings and modes of experience" (Berger and Luckmann 1966:25).

Fine (1983) addresses the social construction of shared fantasy in role playing games. Fantasy is that which is divorced from everyday experience—somehow extraordinary. While participants have the capability to imagine almost anything, "they in fact create only those things that are engrossing and emotionally satisfying. Fantasy is constrained by the social expectations of players and of their world" (Fine 1983:3). As a shared experience, the collective fantasy must be constructed through communication which is only possible when participants share a frame of reference. In the case of renaissance faires and other fantasy medieval settings, that framing comes partially from history, but also from literary sources and popular culture such as Arthurian legend and the works of J.R.R. Tolkien (Cramer 2010). "Everyone gets to pick and choose, to highlight and downplay, the aspects of history that are important to them" (O'Donnell 2004:4).

But why would adults want to become involved in what is in essence a rather elaborate game of make-believe, complete with dress-up? Huizinga states that play is superfluous; it may be suspended at any time while one attends to more pressing matters. It is also not ordinary; it is like stepping out of "real" life and into some other sphere of activity with its own set of rules. And play is secluded within a time and place, separating it from work and responsibility (1950). Taken to the next level, we can see play encompassed within the carnival as Bakhtin (1950) describes it. And indeed, "the Middle Ages occupy a mythic status in Western history" (Cramer 2010:18). Hence, in this carnivalesque context in which any popular media rendition of romantic history might combine with an individual's personal desire to retreat from the stresses of—or perhaps boredom with—their mundane life, it is possible for individuals to construct a consensus fantasy version of the European Renaissance and in doing so become someone else more exciting for a short period of time.

Constructing Community

Cohen writes that "the reality of the community is in its members' perception of the vitality of its culture" (1985:118); that community is symbolically constructed as a source of meaning upon which identities are built. Behavior may be deemed deviant by the responses of others because it defies social norms, and those who commit deviant acts, or represent themselves in a deviant manner, are often treated as "outsiders," leading those who are marginalized socially to create their own norms in liminal social groups or subcultures (Becker 1963). Those individuals who participate in renaissance festivals may often be considered "nerds" or "geeks" by mainstream society (Korol-Evans 2009). There is a certain stigma attached to being the person who prefers to dress up in costume on the weekends and pretend they are knights, princesses, pirates, or some other medieval role which might otherwise seem to belong more to a King Arthur tale than the life of an adult in twenty-first century America (Cramer 2010, O'Donnell 2004). And there is a stereotypical image of the medieval fantasy gamer or science fiction fan who lives in his or her parents' basement, eating junk food and passing up romantic relationships and financial success (Nardi 2010). All of these factors might serve to create a feeling of outsiderdom for avid renfaire participants.

The constructed nature of subculture is particularly evident in the context of the renaissance festival. Korol-Evans' (2009) description of the intrastice, as experienced in the renaissance faire context as a state of existing simultaneously in both the fantasy of the 16th century and the reality of the 21st century, is related to the degree of immersion and the intensity of participation of both performers and playtrons while at the festival. Experience of this intrastice then allows festival participants to express non-normative identity in a socially constructed setting, in which what might otherwise be considered deviant is not so because of the context.

Studies of fan cultures also shed light on participation in renaissance festivals, explaining how the faire provides a forum for those with an affinity for this romanticized version of the historical setting. In fact, media has been found to play a vital role in the formation and maintenance of subcultures (Jancovich 2002). Lacking social or financial success in mainstream culture, fans of knights, pirates, wizards, and other medieval motifs find a way to turn their deficit into an asset in this new setting (Williams 2006).

Identity and Persona

Both Korol-Evans (2009) and Cramer (2010) explore the medieval re-creationist subculture, describing the initiatory process of becoming involved and what factors influence that process. Writing about renaissance festivals, Korol-Evans found that faire attendees "often attend festivals to experience a sense of belonging that perhaps they do not have in their lives outside the faire" (2009:21). Renaissance festivals provide a temporary escape into another reality, a place where participants who seek a more exciting, honorable, or meaningful way of life can find it, even if they must create it themselves in this fantasy context (Cramer 2010, Kim 2004). The magic, as it were, happens in the intrastice, where the boundaries between everyday life and the fantasy realm of the idealized medieval world overlap and blur to suit the needs of the participants (Korol-Evans 2009). In the case of renaissance faires, this takes place most often at festival sites where costumes, props, and all the trappings of the performance are present. As play, all of these trial aspects of alternative identity performance are presumed to be merely temporary—or as temporary as the individual chooses, to be put on and taken off like a mask—and therefore safe within the norms of the carnivalesque context.

Yet, within mainstream society, "ren geeks" as they are sometimes referred to, can find themselves as outsiders, in the way Becker (1963) described other deviant, or at least non-normative, subcultures. "Unsuccessful socialization," as Berger and Luckmann put it, "opens up the question of 'Who am I?'" (1966:171). The outsider as an individualist develops the potential to navigate between the social realms of the everyday and that of the fantasy they prefer to inhabit. He or she deliberately constructs an identity from the cultural archetypes, symbols, and parts of self which exist in both realms which overlap within the faire's intrastice. Though there may not be anything inherently deviant about the generalized archetypal character of a knight, blacksmith, goose girl, or potter, they are still roles which do not readily exist in mainstream American society today, nor do their mode of dress or means of playing their given trades with the possible exception of the occasional craft fair, in the case of the potter. At the same time, chivalry, honor, dependability, and pride in craftsmanship are values which exist in both cultural timeframes (Cramer 2010, O'Donnell 2004)—in the idealization of the sixteenth century and the reality of the twenty-first—to some degree if not in equal measure, helping to create the cultural overlap of the share intrasticive fantasy (Korol-Evans 2009). "When at the same time social structure does not permit the realization of the subjectively chosen identity, an interesting development occurs. The subjectively chosen identity becomes a fantasy identity, objectified within the individual's consciousness as his 'real self'" (Berger and Luckmann 1966:171). Or as Fine writes, "for the game to work as an aesthetic experience players must be willing to 'bracket' their 'natural' selves and enact a fantasy self" (Fine 1983:4). The separateness of the festival grounds, the costumes which are so very different from what is worn in mainstream society, and even the use of character or persona names can aid participants in compartmentalizing what Weitzer would term their "deviant persona" from their "real identity" (2007). For example, though it is not harming anyone for rennies to dress in armor and behave as if they are knights, it is certainly not the sort of thing one expects to encounter on a daily basis. Though by no means detrimentally deviant, such behavior is not the norm, and therefore could be considered deviant for the purpose of sociological study.

Goffman's classic, *The Performance of Self in Everyday Life* (1959), is the canonical basis for studies of social and identity performance, and provides a theoretical basis for exploring the variation in frontstage and backstage identities and interactions, as well as the use of costume, props, and other material culture. However, as appears to be the nature of this subculture, the fantasy element in identity performance (Fine 1983, Korol-Evans 2009, Cramer 2010) leaves many questions concerning how these fantasies are constructed, how they manifest in social groups like the renaissance festival subculture, and even why this social environment in particular is so conducive to their expression.

A new generation of scholars studying recreation and leisure, more specifically fan cultures, assert the importance of fandom in collective behavior and individual identity beyond previous studies of both the rational and emotional components of fandom (Pearson 2007). For the purpose of this study, fandom can be compared with the enthusiasm rennies show for history and tales of medieval adventure in their many forms. "Fans incorporate the cultural texts as part of their self-identity, often going on to build social networks on the basis of shared fandoms" (Pearson 2007:102). So if an individual feels a strong connection with, say, the legends of King Arthur or the latest pirate adventure film, he or she might then seek out a group with similar interests with whom to act out their collective fantasy, adopting a persona which allows them to express their connection to these cultural tropes. Berger and Luckmann might just as well have been describing the renaissance festival subculture when they wrote that "in such a society identities are easily recognizable... Everybody knows who everybody else is... A knight is a knight and a peasant is a peasant, to others as well as to themselves. There is, therefore, no problem of identity" (1966:164). Fine writes that "when animating a character a player must choose between his own self in the guise of the character or playing the self of the character" (1983:4). He is referring to role playing games, but the same concept applies to renaissance festivals and any other type of participatory interactive fan culture. Korol-Evans states that Renaissance festival participants "often portray characters vastly different from their own personalities, allowing them to turn the world upside down and experience the carnivalesque in a visceral manner" (2009:43).

Popular Media's Influence on Identity and Subculture

Mary Bucholtz (2002) writes about youth subculture, as being based on social circumstances rather than chronological age, the long-term, sometimes lifelong engagement in subculture related cultural practices. Many renaissance festival participants and medieval re-creationists continue their involvement into their 40s,

50s, and even later in life (Korol-Evans 2009, Cramer 2010). This engagement in activities often considered the realm of the young is one such example.

Hoelter (1983) found that identity salience depends on commitment to an individual's role in certain social settings, and the importance of the social network group within which those roles are fulfilled, and upon the individual's perception of others' appraisals of their success at certain roles. This in combination with Featherstone and Deflam's (2003) re-examination of Merton's strain theory (Agnew 1997) lends insight into factors which may lead individuals who feel themselves to be outsiders to seek out meaningful social connections within this subculture which romanticizes history and idealizes norms which may vary significantly from those of the dominant culture.

Hoelter describes the main components of identity theory as "role identity, role behavior, and commitment to a particular role" (1983:140). We can define role as a person's position within a group and their actions in the fulfillment of that position—their job within that social context. Identity depends upon the individual's commitment to fulfilling a certain role in a given context, of how important it is to them in defining their self-image. This identity salience can also depend on the number of persons within the social network in which they fulfill a given role, and the intensity of their relationships with others in that group. "Identity salience increases as the degree to which one is committed to the role giving rise to identity increase" (Hoelter 1983:145).

Subculture represents a social setting for expression of facets of identity which may be considered deviant outside its context, a place for individuals to interact through a "common appreciation of myth, make-believe, and freedom of expression" (Goulding and Saren 2009:28). Bucholtz (2002) writes that cultural pressures upon an individual can cause one to respond by seeking out new cultural circumstances which allow for more agency in social behavior and expression of identity. She sees identity as flexible and agentive, with deviant behavior as a "tactical act of identity" (253). "Subcultures constitute alternative systems of shared meaning that take shape precisely by being labeled deviant by members of the dominant culture" (Bucholtz 2002:536). In general strain theory (Agnew 1997), frustration and other negative emotions can constitute the social strain to which an individual then seeks to adapt in a number of ways. One of these adaptations as described by both Merton and Agnew (1997) is retreatism. However, while originally strain theory describes retreatism as a retreat from society or social situation where the strain is incurred, this explanation is not comprehensive and does not apply in all cases of social retreat. I would argue that in the case of subcultures, individuals may indeed be retreating to these social contexts where they feel more comfortable, such as those who flock to the renaissance festival in order to interact with like-minded people.

Although popular, or "fan culture," may often be trivialized as consumer-based and of little relevance, something marketed to teens spending their parents' discretionary income, it is in fact highly agentive. Purchasing decisions equal expression decisions in that what is worn, read, listened to, or otherwise displayed constitute the way by which others read the symbols an individual shows which make up his or her outer self-image (Bucholtz 2002). A person's belongings are the mask he shows society. Subculture, in this case within the setting of the renaissance festival, offers the context for nonnormative, if not necessarily adversely deviant, modes of self-expression. The renaissance festival, with its craftspeople and merchants, offers a meeting of both commercialized yet not mass-produced cultural consumption, as well as a forum for the display of material culture perhaps acquired elsewhere but related in shared meanings to those of the festival context.

Ironically, it is that same institution of popular media which also presents the tools for their transformation, for their formation of an alternative set of goals—in this case of wanting to be something or someone other than what "normal" society dictates. By reading fantasy novels, or watching science fiction or adventure films, or through study of history, or playing certain video or role playing games, the individuals who find their way to the renaissance festival subculture, each in their own way, form a new fanciful self-concept based on these modern manifestations—these popular myths of our time (Campbell 1988)—which they then must find a suitable setting in which to express this alternative identity. By identifying with characters from these stories presented in various media, they come to identify as someone outside of mainstream culture. One way in which we see this is in the romanticized version of history and chivalry as an exotic, seemingly more authentic, ideal for which members of this subculture strive.

Images presented in popular media are adopted by those individuals who then seek to live out the lives they believe they are supposed to have, or simply wish to experience. As Bucholtz points out, they try to live up to the cultural icons they see on the screens and pages which mass media gives them. Media creates and reflects culture, but individuals also add their own sense of self-appropriateness to the parts of that culture they choose to internalize. They borrow adaptations of their own cultural background to create new styles and expressions of identity, with elements from their own heritage selected, appropriated, and manifested in unique ways (Bucholtz 2002). This version of the renaissance provides a kind of resonance with each individual. The resonance exists because of the relative importance such cultural images have within the group narrative, or what Joseph Campbell calls "myths" (1988), which also coincide with members' cultural narratives (Benford and Snow2006). Rennies' various fandoms, their own "nerd heritage" as it were, is an integral part of how narratives and identities are formed through the shared myths of popular fiction and the romanticized version of history which both exist within the subculture's and its haven in the intrasticial setting of the renaissance festival, in the social context where the twenty-first and sixteenth centuries overlap, and fan culture and romanticized history mesh into one cultural tapestry.

Mass media today is in the business of what Edelman (2001) describes as linking brand images to consumer identities. Rojek (2005) concurs that marketing operations present a major force in the power dynamics of consumer culture and how leisure is practiced. Branding has become intertwined with culture, space, and identities that even rennies put forth great personal financial investment to buy things which coincide with their fandom or express the identity they want to convey.

Expressions of collective identity with a community, such as the "subculture ideology through which fan cultures produce a sense of identity through their supposed difference from the 'mainstream'" (Jancovich 2002:306) can be forces in non-normative individual identity formation. Jancovich argues that, despite their unique ideology, such subcultures are not self-generated from within and later encroached upon by the media, but instead mass media's imagery and popular mythos are central to both their formation and continuation. What might be collectively termed "nerd culture," of which many fandoms and unique subcultures such as renaissance faires are a part, shows signs of similar practices and collective ideologies.

It is certainly possible to consider the renaissance festival subculture in this light, noting its unique ideologies, preferred types of products, and fandom affinities in order to create another niche market. Style for subcultures becomes a "form of lived contestation and innovation" (Stahl 1999:7), or to use a present-day colloquialism, a way of "letting one's freak flag fly" or expressing individual difference from what is commonly accepted. It is a process which may be also used by the dominant culture in an attempt to convert subcultural signs into commodities and the relabeling of deviant behavior by making it marketable. Style within subculture—in this case a historical if fanciful one—is a symbolic response to exclusion from the parent culture. While it is not a "real" solution to feelings of outsiderdom, it does serve as another strand to strengthen the bonds of group solidarity within the subculture, and to differentiate group goals from those of the mainstream culture. To the uninitiated, the renaissance faire may seem little more than "a costume party, a masquerade, a hedonistic escape into...a fantasy characterized by political indifference" (Stahl 1999:13). Costumed, yes; indifferent, no.

Methods

I conducted my research with the intent of answering several specific research questions. How is the shared fantasy of romanticized history constructed at renaissance festivals and in the "rennie" subculture that exists within that context? How do participants become interested and involved in this subculture? How is identity performed in the renaissance festival setting? To what degree participation in renaissance festivals and affiliation with this subculture affect participants' lives outside of the renaissance faire? The purpose of this paper is to find answers to these key questions within a framework of sociological theory.

Data Collection and Coding

Data collection for this project consisted of participant observation combined with in-depth interviews with festival participants in various roles within the subculture. Renfaires take place during a "season" which may be from a single weekend to perhaps two months or more at a time, with gates open to visitors only on the weekends during that period of time. I traveled to two different festival sites in the region, spending the majority of the faire season weekends on site collecting data. In all I spent 12 weekends between June and October at my research sites, sometimes camping at the festival campgrounds with those faire workers who lived on site to gain a better understanding of their experiences. Because of the participatory nature of this subculture, it was necessary for me to spend some time in attendance on site at one or more of these festivals, observing with a sociologist's eye, instead of trying to merely survey participants outside of this context. Being in this context not only gave me a ready pool of potential interviewees but also let me observe a cross section of the population who take part in renaissance faires in many different roles, something which I later came to understand is quite meaningful.

Data collected in the form of extensive field notes, photographs, and interview transcripts was examined using analytic induction. Open coding involved paying special attention to themes involving identity performance and the social construction of shared fantasy. Further, more specific coding was then done to refine themes such as participants' roles within the festival subculture, costume and other aspects of identity performance, and mention of stigma outside the renaissance faire context. Using this process, and with my research questions in mind, as new data was collected throughout this study, new information was constantly compared to earlier data collected and coded according to those aforementioned themes and emerging patterns. The progressive redefinition of concepts based on emerging patterns in the data in light of my theoretical framing. As more cases were added, hypotheses were either modified based on the new data or else re-categorized as new emergent patterns. Following data collection, the analysis of the data included explicit coding of the qualitative data and theoretical development induced from this method of constant comparison.

While the bulk of my data was collected in the form of interviews and field notes, I also took copious photographs while on site at the renaissance festivals I attended while conducting this study. The purpose of these was to capture the visual effects of the setting as well as to record minute details which might I might otherwise not be able to record fast enough while taking notes, such as the variety of costumes and certain demographics of participants, such as apparent age, race, or level of immersion based on mode of dress, among the thousands of people on site with whom I was not able to interact. Through use of my own notes and the analysis of these photographs I was able to construct a picture of the overall population of those who participate in renaissance festivals on some level, at least within the region where I conducted my study. In this case, a picture really was worth a thousand words. The photographs served to supplement my written field notes, allowing me to capture entire scenes rich with data instantaneously and fully, at least visually, without the need for me to stop and try to write down every detail, leaving me free to note interactions and things participants said. I was also able to use the photos to supplement demographic information, as well as to reference such details as costumes and scene.

Data Sites

I traveled to two renaissance festivals in the region, and though a more thorough examination of renaissance faires is sure to be had by extending that to other festivals, time and travel expenses limited my own project to these two. One faire was the Kentucky Highland Renaissance Festival (KHRF), at which I was welcomed by the cast and management, and allowed free run of the site for my research purposes. The second, which I will refer to using the pseudonym of the Queen's Renaissance Festival (QRF), is one where I had previously made a number of contacts during some informal research as an undergraduate student, but was not able to gain permission from the management to mention this particular faire by name.

The KHRF season runs from the first weekend of June through mid-July, Saturdays and Sundays only. I traveled to this festival site each of the six weekends in order to conduct interviews and participant observation at this faire. I was able to secure overnight tent camping accommodations on site at the Highland faire one of the six weekends, during which time I was privileged to be part of the cast's camp and see what goes on in that backstage portion of the festival. QRF's season was early September through late October, again weekends only. I made the trip each of the eight weekends the festival is open, again for participant observation and interviews. Weekend overnight accommodations for this site were not available at the festival grounds, but on occasion were proffered by some of my contacts from this location to stay with them in their homes. This more mundane setting among the members of this subculture, presented its own specific insights into the culture.

As a participant observer, I sought to fit in with the subculture, dressing in renaissance costume as a means to more completely integrate into the social context and build rapport with my research subjects. Ethnographic research of this kind can lend authenticity to the lived experiences of participants in immersive communities through the lens of social science theory. I would not have received the same in-depth responses if I had arrived in plain clothes, clipboard and recorder in hand, expecting to get an insider's view of a dynamic social setting which is based so fully in a participatory shared fantasy. If I had not showed willingness to play along, it would have seemed condescending; therefore I joined in, carrying a leather-bound notebook in which to record my notes as part of my garb. I was not disappointed by the reception I received.

Interviews and Sample Selection

This study is largely exploratory and consisted of open-ended interviews intended to learn how participants became involved in this subculture and what factors influence their participation and identity expression, both in and outside of the renaissance festival setting. In addition to the data collected in my own field notes, I also interviewed some of the participants using a set of open-ended questions as a flexible interview guide. While the interview guide was a basis of my inquiries, I tried to allow each informant to tell me their own story and personal experiences whenever possible, with some direction on my part in order to obtain information pertinent to my research questions. Thus the exact format and information gleaned from each interview varied somewhat due to this more conversational approach.

Potential informants were approached at the respective festival sites and introduced to the nature of my study, then asked for verbal consent to participate in the interview. Interviews were conducted at the respondents' convenience at a secluded location within the festival grounds. Scheduling was sometimes tricky because many of the individuals I interviewed were working at the festivals in various roles, either as part of the street cast or shopkeepers with one of the on-site businesses, and not only could not stop to speak to me at length while working, but also were quite often not allowed to break character within sight of visitors lest they spoil the fantasy.

All in all I conducted 21 formal interviews involving 38 individuals, as some of the sessions involved more than one person, such as the breakfast meeting I was able to arrange with the entire jousting troupe, with seven members present, at KHRF. Others, such as one married couple and more than one performing duo, also were only able to schedule an interview as a pair due to the nature of their working role while on site. I also conducted some 40 more brief informal interviews and countless conversations with participants in a myriad of roles while in attendance.

Nearly all of my interviewees have a character or persona name which they use while at renaissance faires, and some of them even perform a stage act under those names. In the case of the stage performers, they each individually stated that they prefer that I use their stage names and include the name of their stage act in any academic writings in which I make reference to them. Therefore, I shall do so here. When interview subjects indicated that they prefer I should refer to them as their actual faire persona or character name, I do so; all other names are pseudonyms to protect the anonymity of my informants.

Interview subjects were chosen with the intention of capturing as representative a sample as might be possible of a certain sub-section of renaissance festival participants. Yet the sample was still influenced by considerations of who was willing to participate and how much time they might have available to speak with me. While several thousand visitors might attend a given renfaire during each season, many of them are only there as tourists—referred to simply as "patrons"—or those people who attend in regular street clothes as one might visit any theme park. Those were not the individuals I sought to study. I meant to look deeper into the social phenomenon of the renfaire at those individuals who work there or choose to dress in costume and take part in the interaction as if they are also part of the constructed reality of that context. Those who work at the faire fall into a few main categories, those of street cast who portray the nobility and villagers who make up the context of the festival, the stage performers, and the shopkeepers who are often referred to as "boothies." Those people who pay for admission to the faire site and choose to wear a renaissance costume and play along as part of the fantasy are called "playtrons," meaning patrons who play.

It is these more immersive categories of persons,

playtrons, performers, and others who are part of the fantasy construct that is the renaissance festival, with whom my study is concerned. And I set about selecting interview subjects to best represent a cross section of the individuals in these roles within this context. Some of my interviewees fulfill multiple roles, such as being both stage performers and street cast, or being a playtron at one faire and a boothie at another.

We might wish to inquire who renaissance festival participants are, demographically speaking. Two afternoons of data collection at both research sites with this specific question in mind yielded an overall picture of the age and racial makeup of renaissance faire visitors in the region (Table 1). Based on appearances, while this is an event attended by all ages, most attendees are young adults in their 20s and 30s, with teenagers and 40-somethings or even older also well represented. Those present were overwhelmingly Caucasian. And though no one of a minority race agreed to speak to me about why this might be, I hypothesize that it may be at least partially due to the theme of the venue itself being that of the European Renaissance, specifically Scotland and England respectively at the two site I visited, and may not have the same resonance with cultural heritage that the event has for those of British and other European descent.

Also of note, and somewhat counter to stereotypes of fantasy and science fiction fandom as a male-dominated genre (Nardi 2010, Williams 2006), were the very balanced numbers with regard to gender. In fact, I counted 412 females—women and girls—and 388 males (Table 1) during this phase of the project. This is by no means the total number of people in attendance on any given day of either festival, which might number between 5,000 and 12,000 depending on the site, the weather, and particular events such as concerts or highland games that might be happening on various themed weekends.

Table 1

Observed Demographics of Renaissance Festival Attendees

Age		Race		Gender		Dress	
Child	48	White	790	Male	388	Full Costume	394
Teen	146	African Am.	7	Female	412	Partial Costume	127
20s	234	Asian	3			Non-Ren. Costume	8
30s	207					Mundane	270
40s	110						
50s	44						
60+	11						

Total Sample   800

Note: This sample was collected by a simple head count of apparent age, race, gender, and whether or to what degree participants were dressed in costume.

Results

I began this project with a few basic questions in mind. How is the shared fantasy of romanticized history constructed at renaissance festivals and within the "rennie" subculture? How do participants become interested and involved in this subculture? How is identity performed in the renaissance festival setting? What influences the construction of these presumably alternate or non-normative identity performances, and how do they differ from identities performed outside the festival or the subculture? And to what degree participation in renaissance festivals and affiliation with this subculture affect participants' lives outside of the renaissance faire? In the process of analytic induction, other themes emerged from the data, such as the strong sense of belonging that so many participants experience, the driving impetus between fantasy and identity depending upon an individual's role within the festival context.

Constructing the Fantasy

One of my initial questions was to examine how the shared fantasy of romanticized history is constructed at renaissance festivals and within the "rennie" subculture. There are two sides from which to explore this question; one is that of those people who work at the festival, the other is from the viewpoint of the playtrons who attend in order to mingle their personal fantasies with that of the faire through their interactions with others who are also playing within the similar theme. For the first part, I spent most of the season at the Kentucky Highland Renaissance Festival (KHRF) with the members of the street cast and other performers at this festival talking to them and observing what they do to make the faire come to life.

Cast auditions take place in early March, with rehearsals most every weekend from then until the festival opens the first weekend of June. The cast director, who goes by Caro the Piper during the faire season, described the audition process to me. "We ask them to do a monologue. We ask them to sing Happy Birthday. And then we ask them to do some improv with a straight man," she said. This is to give the directors a feel for the person's acting and singing ability, as well as how they can think on their feet without the benefit of a prepared script. "This is an improv cast," Caro said. Most of their performance throughout the nine-hour faire day involves interacting with patrons and each other while remaining in character.

There is a bit of type casting in choosing what character each cast member will portray. Some are actual historical figures, such as King Robert the Bruce or Queen

Elizabeth. Others are simply historically plausible nobles, tradespeople, and peasants who populate the village. The assistant cast director, who plays a pirate captain and goes by the name of Captain Amos, explained that "as they start to build their character we get them to start building garb. And the garb reflects their station." Garb is the term used for costume in this subculture, intending to show the difference between a costume, which is a fanciful garment intended to be worn only temporarily, and practical clothing of a quality to be worn over and over again—something to be lived in—as more befitting of what is worn by most experienced renaissance faire participants. "And we do typecast," Caro said. Capt. Amos pointed out that it is easier to stay in character all day if that character is a great deal like one's own personality already.

Once characters are assigned, there is a process of acclimating to the role. One cast member, who goes by the faire name of Lady Sersha, said:

> "For the people coming in who are reprising their role it's a little less intensive. And it's our job to coach the new people. When you first come in, several ideas are tossed around during your first rehearsal. We try to find, for the new people, characters that will fit within the existing framework, who also bring something new. For instance, this year we brought in a butcher and a cooper. We try to develop a character within that framework and look for historically plausible characters."

One case of this character development came in the person of Oona McGee, a new cast member who took on the role of the goose girl. I had known Oona for a couple of years as a playtron prior to her auditioning for the cast of KHRF. During that time, she was studying theatre in college and expressed her enjoyment for the various costumes she was able to create and wear to the faire. However, until taking on the goose girl character, Oona's performance of identity had been inconsistent, changing sometimes daily while at the renaissance festival depending on which costume she chose to wear that day, from pirate wench, to fancy Elizabethan lady, to hyper-masculinized warrior in homage to her favorite science fiction series involving pirates in outer space. I believe that she was exploring facets of identity through these performances, anchored by the outward manifestation of the clothing she wore, as she conveyed to me as we conversed while she waited for her turn to audition for the KHRF cast.

Oona did not learn until the next week that she had been chosen to be part of the faire's cast. And did not choose a specific character until the first time the cast met for rehearsals, which were more like acting workshops than practice for a play because of the fluid, improvisational nature of the acting involved. Because of Oona's own self-concept of being a bit absent-minded and more than a little gullible, she eventually settled into the peasant role as the village goose girl, as one who would be left to tend the various barnyard fowl and keep them safe from harm—"like a shepherd, but for geese," she said. Over the next two months, she created a simple costume to wear as the goose girl, consisting of a simple gown and apron-like over-tunic, and topped off with a straw hat to protect her from the summer sun. For props she carried a basket which usually held three plush toy geese. Her geese had names, and during the faire she pretended they were her pets, much to the delight of many of the younger patrons. As the goose girl, a kindhearted jokester emerged in how she played the character, with her mischief often blamed on the geese.

In Oona's case, as with the other performers, the collective fantasy of the faire itself—that of the romanticized renaissance village on a festival day—held supremacy over the way the character she portrayed was performed. The shared fantasy of the renfaire, no matter the specific scenario of each individual festival site, already exists in its general form for all those who participate. In that sense the fantasy is static. One might attend any renaissance festival across the country and encounter a similar subculture, with the same types of stage acts, a joust, shops and booths selling the same types of merchandise, and people dressed in renaissance costumes intermingled and interacting with plain clothes patrons.

However, because of the improvisational nature of the interactions themselves, the fantasy is also emergent. Each participant adds to any interaction, whether between performers, playtrons, patrons, or any combination, depending on the situation and the action and dialog happening at the time. One lunch resulted in my own being sent to the stocks after a rather comical argument with the Town Crier about whether the French fries I was eating were turnips or "tatties" (Scottish slang for potatoes). The incident started when Natasha, the Russian dancer, took and ate one of the fries and I tried to chase after her. Luckily, I was able to talk the Constable out of making me stand in the stocks by having one of "my minions," that being a playtron with whom I was eating lunch, stand there in my stead. This episode illustrates the emergent nature of the interactions encountered at every turn on a typical faire day, and thus the emergent nature of the interactive, daily part of the fantasy as well, unscripted and based on the creativity of the individuals involved.

But it is not just a matter of having a well-trained street cast. The site itself, the physical setting, also goes through a transformation in order to create the fantasy. "I think the site itself creates it first. What we do is create a place for the people to come, the cast and crew and the patrons, and they actually create the atmosphere itself," said Ed Frederick, general manager and part-owner at KHRF. Being a relatively new festival, in its seventh season during the time I was doing my research for this project, the process of creating the fantasy context of the faire grounds was still fresh enough to grant stories from several of the individuals who had been working there since that first season.

"When my wife and I first walked down what is now Main Street, this was a corn field," Frederick said. Capt. Amos shared a colorful tale about how it had rained for several days before the first opening day, leaving the paths a veritable "mud hole" when the visitors arrived. The first year all the shops were set up in large pavilion tents, and the main pub, now a great hall seven years later, was also only a tent. Little by little, year by year, new buildings, shops, and stages were built. The addition of a faerie land grove was the new attraction, with several members of the cast portraying winged faeries and other fae creatures.

In addition to the physical grounds and the cast of

villagers, the paths are lined with shops where vendors and craftspeople sell all manner of renaissance themed merchandise. And then there are stage performers whose acts might be anything from singing to juggling, sword fighting to fire eating. Not to mention the joust, to some the main attraction of any renfaire, as festivals at that time in history were often centered around tournaments of horsemanship and the combat arts. Men and women in full plate armor ride full-tilt, which is where the phrase comes from, at targets and sometimes each other. Their impact carries more than 3,000 lbs. of force per square inch, according to the master of ceremonies for the QRF's joust.

All of these processes in conjunction serve to remove as much of the 21st century as possible and replace it with the semblance of life in the European Renaissance, or at least the good, romantic parts of it. "The weather, the dust, and the smell are all entirely authentic," Lee Bishop, boothie and sometimes pirate commodore playtron, said to passing patrons while hocking the wares of the shop at which he was employed for the season at QRF. "All this is a big form of escapism, and that's what makes it so popular," manager Ed Frederick said of KHRF. That escape from the mundane world and into the fantasy of the renfaire involves taking on an alternate identity to some degree, for those who participate beyond the level of tourist patrons.

Becoming the Persona

I was especially curious about how participants become interested and involved in this activity and subculture. And as I asked them to tell me their stories, invariably the development of the faire persona was part of the process of integration into the subculture. Coupled with the development of this alternate, dare I say non-normative, identity, there emerged in many of their stories the theme of experiencing a strong sense of belonging which participants spoke of not feeling anywhere except at the renaissance faire or among their rennie friends. "I felt so at home here," a long-time renfaire participant calling herself Jezzie the Pirate Queen described her first experience at the renaissance festival. "I can talk about the things that I like, and wear the kind of clothes I like, and no one laughs at me for it. At faire I'm with people who accept me for who I am," a woman called Oona said. "I call them my faire-mily," said another woman dressed as a pirate. In fact, the faerie troupe, a subgroup of the street cast at the Kentucky Highland Renaissance Festival, call themselves the Faewood Faemily, again playing on the word family and demonstrating the importance of their sense of belonging within the group.

I was privileged to observe one new playtron during his first visit to a renaissance festival. At the age of 29, he was already an avid gamer, in both MMORPGs and tabletop RPGs like Dungeons & Dragons. In fact, he chose to wear a t-shirt to his first day at KHRF with the emblem of his favorite faction from World of Warcraft. After the first lap around the village, getting a glimpse at the variety of the shops and taking in the atmosphere, cries of, "For the

Horde!" rung out a total of six times. "That's number six," he said smiling, after another battle cry came from one of the vendor's tents, "These are my people." This small affirmation was the impetus it took for this man to seek out a deeper immersion in the experience. By the end of the day, he had traded his shorts for a kilt, and acquired a leather belt and sporran (Scottish belt pouch worn with a kilt), a tam style hat, "goblin" ears, and a studded wooden cudgel. He even came up with a name to call himself while dressed as this new persona—a Goblin Prince. Most certainly the fantasy gaming background was an influence upon the decision to take on the goblin character. And he did not exchange the t-shirt for a more historically appropriate shirt until his next trip to a renaissance faire later in the year. However, by that point without the rubber ears the rest of the costume needed only some historically accurate shoes, in this case knee-high suede moccasins, to be plausible renaissance garb.

The transformation from new patron to renaissance festival playtron and devotee was dramatic and quick in this case, because of the sense of belonging this man experienced during his initial exposure to the setting and interaction with members of the subculture. It should be noted that more than $200 was spent on his transformation that first day, and more money at later visits to faires after that. Because these items of clothing and accessories are not readily available in mainstream venues and are often hand made by independent artisans, costume pieces can be costly. Thus individuals with more expendable financial resources would be able to accumulate a larger wardrobe of appropriate pieces more quickly. While changes in attitude and outlook can happen almost instantly, the costume may take longer. And it would be interesting to study, in the future, a more in-depth look at this transformation process itself, with attention to how much the outward trappings which express the internal identity each individual is trying to convey have a bearing upon the degree to which they feel they belong in the subculture.

Other participants described similar feelings of belonging during their first experiences at renaissance faires. "After about 40 paces inside the gate I said, 'I'm home!' And I fell in love," said one performer, a woman who has made a career of singing in a renfaire stage show with her sister, and working at faires around the country for more than 20 years. This story repeats itself among so many of the playtrons and performers. "I fell in love with the faire. Within an hour I was completely dressed [in renaissance garb] head to toe," another woman, a boothie, described her first experience at a renaissance festival.

Some participants, playtrons and performers both, have described a certain faire as "home." For example, the gentleman who has been my guide since the beginning of my research in the subculture said of KHRF after his first visit, "[QRF] is my work faire. I work there, I know the people there. But Kentucky is where I go to relax. This is the home soil." And he told a story about his pirate crew claiming a picnic table. "We had a flag and everything." Some of the stage performers mentioned that their home faire was in Texas, or Maryland, or northern Ohio, depending on what part of the country they hailed from. Over and over again there was talk of the renaissance festival feeling like home, like there was acceptance and room for safe expression there that was not allowed out in the real world.

> "I have learned a lot about self-acceptance. I feel like I fit in here. The only way I know how to relate to and interact with in the outside world is as the Weird One. I'm a pharmacy tech, and I've had people in my professional life look at me and say, 'Where did you come from?' I tell them I came from the renaissance festival. It does not matter how hard I try, I cannot force myself to fit in with the outside world like I do here," Natasha said.

Every participant, whether performer or playtron, has a story about the process by which they created and assumed their alternate identity. For Natasha, it all started with learning a Russian accent and then building a character around a romantic version of that culture. For some it is a matter of being able to embody an aspect of their core self which they felt unable to do to their satisfaction elsewhere. "I feel as though a part of me has always been a faerie," said Oakley, the director of the faerie troupe. And Lee, the Commodore, said, "I'm a pirate at heart." While neither faerie nor pirate is a viable identity in mainstream society, those things were able to come to light within the shared fantasy context of the renaissance festival, particularly because of the consensus understanding that the faire is a safe place to do so, and that acceptance of others' personal fantasy identities without stigma is one of the defining aspects of the subculture itself.

No matter the specific archetypal character portrayed in each individual's persona, many individuals mentioned costume as a defining part of their identity performance while at the faire. Luna, a playtron in her late 20s, said, "It's the corset. I get mostly dressed at home and then drive to the faire site. But when I get out of the car and lace up the bodice, that's when the wench comes out. That's when it feels real." Another example, this one a stage performer and member of the street cast, Capt. Amos, said that the most important aspect of his garb is his hat. "I love that hat! From the end of Main Street down there, they know that I'm the Captain." Many of the playtrons joked about the Captain's "magic hat." As a very charismatic personality and a musician, Amos is very popular, and not a few hours would go by on any day of the festival before some young woman or teenage girl would take his hat and walk away wearing it. He would always insist that they return it by the time of his next stage show. "I can't get up and sing without it," he said. "It's like leaving the house without your pants. I'm just not right without my hat."

Many participants, especially the playtrons, were influenced by popular media in the creation of their personal fantasy identities and thus the personae they choose to portray. In recent years there have been a string of pirate adventure films, making pirates a popular theme among playtrons despite the fact that they are slightly out of sync historically with the timeframe of many festivals. The anachronisms are themselves part of the culture of the faire. Others are influenced by their own cultural heritage, as in the case of quite a few participants from the region which has a large population of people of Irish and Scottish descent. Kilts are popular at the renaissance faire with those of Celtic and non-Celtic descent alike.

In looking at how identity is performed in the renaissance festival setting, and what influences the construction of these presumably alternate or non-normative identity performances, it is important to note the interplay between the shared fantasy of the faire itself and the personal fantasy of the persona. During this project, two distinct processes emerged depending upon the individual's role within the context of the faire—whether they are a playtron or a performer, that being a stage performer, cast member, or even to some extent boothies—and whether identity created the shared fantasy or the fantasy context informed the facets of identity which emerged in interaction.

Identity and Roles
in the Renaissance Festival

The renfaire participants who truly take part in the shared fantasy can be divided into two basic categories, those of performers and playtrons. "Playtrons," or patrons who play along, pay the ticket price to get into the faire where they are dressed in costume and interact with each other, the performers, and other patrons as the character of their chosen persona, to one degree or another. The group I am referring to collectively as "performers" are all those people who work at renaissance faire while in character to some extent, and can be divided into three subcategories of stage performers, street cast, and "boothies."

Boothies is the rennie term used for the shopkeepers and craftspeople who work in the various booths at the festival. They all dress in costume and portray some kind of character, even if it is merely that of a renaissance merchant, which is quite common. Theirs is a performance which requires that they be able to easily incorporate a mild intrasticive state—the overlap of the sixteenth and twenty-first centuries—in which they do not detract from the fantasy of the renaissance era festival day, but at the same time they are able to sell merchandise, handle cash, and process credit card payments through applications on their cell phones. One may often see signage which reads, "Lady Visa and Master Card accepted here," which illustrates this point. The role of the boothies is ultimately driven by the conducting of their business, but that business relies on the guests' enjoyment of the fantasy context, therefore causing the vendors to have to walk the fine line between being both in and out of the fantasy.

"I use the term 'merchant adventurer' because when I'm not selling something I like to travel," said Stephen, a boothie who owns a women's clothing shop that exists only at various renfaires. He described himself as "merchant class," both in and outside of the festival, citing a day job through the week as the thing that both affords his ability to run his boot at the renaissance festival and to travel the world on vacation. But he said that when he is working in his shop at the festival, there is a lot of acting involved, both in making a sale and adding to the shared fantasy of the venue. "I perform a short play called 'Sale of a Corset,' but I perform it about 200 times a day. Sometimes it's semi scripted, sometimes it's off-the-cuff. It's fun because it lets me interact with the patrons." Stephen also finds that his role as a vendor and the products he sells add to the collective fantasy. "I think that adding to the beauty of the festival is important, so the more people in costume the better, the more the feeling that you're there. I like to encourage people to dress up, even if they don't buy anything from me."

For most performers, the creation of the fantasy itself is their job. The degree to which visitors are about to suspend their disbelief and play along, to experience that intrasticive state of shared fantasy, depends a great deal on how well the people working at the renfaire are able to carry off that performance. Capt. Amos described how, in order to do so, cast members must themselves believe the fantasy to some extent. At KHRF the back gate through which all festival workers enter the site is referred to among the cast as the "portal."

> "When I walk through the Portal, I am the Captain. I'm not [myself] portraying the Captain. I am the Captain. That's where I make that huge leap from playing a role to being this character. And that's the only way to do it when you're here for a 12 hour day. It's so hard to stay in character if you are playing a role. But if, once you walk in and you put the hat on, you feel like you are that, then it's not staying in character, you just are who you are."

The kind of lengthy performance in character which the street cast members do brings out an element of the individual's own personal identity that manifests in aspects of the character they play. Every single cast member with whom I spoke used the phrase "yourself turned up to 11" when describing their identity while in character. And many of them talked about there being some article of clothing, like the Captain's hat, or the costume itself which also made them feel as if they were stepping into that persona more completely. In their case, the context informs the character. Who they become is largely driven by how that character fits into the scenario of the faire's theme, their status within the festival itself, or the nature of the show they perform in.

It is also notable that some performers spoke of their characters in the third person, with a sense of detachment, even though they said the character was their own personality amplified. The stage performers are commonly referred to as "paid entertainers" or simply entertainers, and afforded a position of relative privilege in the hierarchy of those working at the renfaire. All of the entertainers I interviewed made the distinction between when they were in or out of character. The members of the street cast I interviewed seemed to vary as to whether they spoke about their character in the first or third person. I observed that whether they acted as if they were fully in character when interacting did seem to determine the difference in whether they referred to the character they portrayed as "I" or "s/he." In some cases, such as the stage performers who go by the names George Silver and Rocco Bonetti, who make up the comedy sword fighting act the Dueling Fools, their characters were not just created for the show itself, but were actual historical persons whom they have adapted for their act. "Rocco Bonetti the historical figure is nothing like my representation of him," said the man portraying this character on stage, whom I still refer to as Rocco. Later his stage partner referred to his representation of the historical personage in the form of his character in the third person, saying, "Silver thinks he is better than everyone." Stage performer Doktor Kaboom said of creating his character, "I built him at renaissance festivals," almost as if his stage character is an object he crafted. In such cases the degree of internalization of the character is much less than with playtrons who create their persona out of their ideal selves. As one young man put it, "It's whatever I want to be."

Whereas more often than not—in perhaps half of the more than 50 total individuals I interviewed over the course of this study, asking them even briefly about their persona—the playtrons spoke of their faire persona in the first person, saying "I" and "me." They treated the alternative identity as the self they were performing at that time, as either an integrated part of themselves or at least as who they wished to be treated as at the moment. "I'm a little bit not-dirty greasy pirate," Captain Amos described himself at faire. Another renfaire pirate, Crystiana, introduced herself to another playtron in the parking lot outside the festival grounds, "I'm the captain of the Bloody Compass." "I'm the goose girl! I sometimes act a little...goosey," Oona exclaimed. She went so far as to call her father Pa McGee, using her character's surname, on the day her parents visited the faire.

In the case of most playtrons, their personal fantasy, that of a more authentic or ideal self which they may feel unable to portray outside the renfaire because of social stigma, socioeconomic constraints, relationship complications, or a myriad of other factors, not the least of which being that our 21st century society simply has very little place for pirates and princesses. Through the romanticized version of history that exists in the renaissance festival, these facets of identity can come to life and step into the world to interact with others—the truest form of play.

There is a social construction of reality which I refer to as consensus identity. That is, as it has been said more than once by renfaire participants in what could be interpreted as a reiteration of the Thomas Theorem, "if you say you're it, and no one says you're not it, then you're it." Or as Goffman (1959) might have put it, the audience's acceptance of the individual's identity, as announced by his or her costume, behavior, or other cues. Simply put, Lee is the Commodore of a pirate fleet, despite neither he nor any of his friends even owning a boat, because they all agree that he is one—that they all are in fact pirates, at least within the context of the faire. They dress as pirates, speak like them to some extent, and even organize their extended clique into various ships' crews complete with flags as a way of fleshing out their identities, both individually and collectively. They are each one another's audience in their performance of their alternative identities and of the shared fantasy in which they take part. And the other rennies treat this bunch as if they are pirates. The goodwyfe, Mistress Seely Guillie, from KHRF's street cast repeatedly called Lee out for being a "scurvy pirate," as it is part of her persona to "make sure people are doing what they're supposed to," as she put it in an in-character interview. For playtrons, the fantasy persona or idealized self is what informs identity performance. Others then interact with them in this consensus of identity that is the shared social fantasy.

Outside the Festival

The last of my original research questions involves how and to what degree participation in renaissance festivals and affiliation with this subculture affects participants' lives outside of the renaissance faire. This can be looked at on many levels, including those of finances, social stigma, and identity.

It was interesting to note how many people dressed in renaissance costume, since that is one of the surest signs of attempted integration with the subculture and willingness to share in the collective fantasy of the faire. Almost exactly half of all individuals observed were dressed in full renaissance costume (Table 1), although that figure does include any workers or performers present as well, not just visitors, since it is sometimes difficult to distinguish festival workers from playtrons without asking the individual. Approximately 16 percent more attempted some partial costume, perhaps an accessory or single piece of garb with their street clothes. There were also a handful of people who wore some other non-renaissance costume. One gentleman arrived in a Star Trek uniform, and seven individuals were observed wearing costumes depicting characters from the British television program Doctor Who. This might seem out of place to someone unfamiliar with these television programs, but when one considers that in those story lines the heroes travel in time and visit other planets, it seems entirely plausible, when one delves into that fantasy, that they might encounter a setting very much like a village in renaissance Europe on a festival day. Beyond that were left the remaining one third of people present as visitors in plain clothes' who were in no way the subject of this study, as they were essentially tourists there for the spectacle of it all.

It is difficult, without asking directly, to discern socioeconomic status of festival attendees, especially those who dress in costume. And it was beyond the original research questions of this project to do so. KHRF general manager Ed Frederick, himself a horse trainer when he is not running the renaissance festival, mentioned that there are all manner of well-to-do professionals, "doctors and lawyers," who attend renaissance faires, to show that it is a venue for respectable families and not merely the party crowd. It was my impression that, as a business owner and festival manager, one of his primary concerns is the success of the faire as a tourist attraction. As such, he seeks to legitimize the event in the eyes of the public by pointing out that this is a safe activity which the whole family can enjoy, thus wanting to put a nice, middle class face on things. My own interviews and casual conversations with festival attendees and workers alike yielded a more modest socio-economic demographic among the rennies I spoke with, giving me the impression that especially the playtrons and performers are more of a working class group overall. I met restaurant and retail managers, pharmacy techs, forklift drivers, waitresses, DJs, sales people, cashiers, teachers, stay-at-home mothers, and one college professor just to name a few. There were also a notable segment of the people I spoke with who made a point to tell me that "rennies are very educated," as one boothie told me. Another shop owner said that "you'll find more master's degrees per capita at the faire than almost anywhere else." While I doubt that was not an empirical statement, he did continue to point to each shop and booth along the lane and tell me a list of people working there and what manner college degrees they were reputed to hold. So while there are a wide range of jobs and careers represented, especially among the playtrons and street cast, the generalization I would make is more that of educated but working class. Though this is certainly a matter that would warrant closer examination in future studies.

At first it would seem that some vague guess about socioeconomic status might be made based on the quality or perceived expense of each individual's clothing or garb, but that is not the case. Since wearing renaissance garb is one of the most tangible, outward means of expression of the alternate identity that is part of the attraction of the faire itself, participants are usually willing to put more money and effort into their costumes than they would into other items. One of the popular items of clothing, among the group of playtrons with whom I spent a great deal of time, were some very elaborate patchwork skirts for the ladies. Each of these skirts, made up of hundreds of small bits of brightly colored fabric hand sewn together in such a way as to flare out into nearly a full circle when the wearer twirls around, is then dyed in a color bath to give the entire garment an overall hue. Each skirt retails for $144. And the ladies wear them with other layers of skirts, blouses, and tightly laced bodices which can cost more than $100 each, not to mention boots, hats, belts, and other accessories. The cost of a costume can add up quickly. I even observed four separate individuals who chose to ignore utility bills and grocery costs in favor of purchasing that one special item—be it sword, skirt, or other accessory—that they desired to go with their garb.

"I can pick up an extra shift or two this week at [the restaurant] to cover this. The electric is due by Thursday," one young woman said while justifying how to pay for one of those patchwork skirts. It would seem that because the emotional connection is greater, the willingness to sacrifice outside financial obligations for faire purchases is also higher. Again, this is a question that could be examined in greater detail in future studies.

Festival attendance itself can be costly, with tickets averaging $20 a day, plus the cost of food and beverages while inside the faire, and gas and travel costs. Not to mention that some more elaborate costumes can ring in at a total price tag of more than a thousand dollars.

But there are more than just financial concerns involved in the real world implications of renaissance festival participation. Spending so much time interacting as an alternate identity can have an effect on an individual's behavior in mainstream society as well, as attested to by Phillip McGuinness, who is the "town drunk" half of the singing pirate duo Drunk & Sailor, along with Capt. Amos, spoke about how much his character and his real world self are integrated.

> "When you play the same character year after year, you want a character that is easy for you to get into because you're going to be that character for hours and hours. But what I did not expect was after a while Phillip started to come into me too. I'm not an alcoholic by any stretch of the imagination. I was never a beer snob or anything like that before either. But I am now, I think, because of Phillip."

Phillip and the Captain perform as Drunk & Sailor

outside of the renaissance festival at various bars, pubs, and other festivals throughout the years. Aspects of the character surfaced in the real world identity by fact of interacting with others as that character for such a large portion of the time.

Discussion

"This is the real world; the rest of it's the imaginary part. I go to work and sit there at my desk, and I exist. Then I come here on the weekends and this is where I feel really alive," Phillip McGuinness said at the close of an especially hot summer Saturday at KHRF. The renaissance festival takes on an idealized setting where ladies curtsey and gentlemen all speak politely, even the roguish ones. Some participants view the faire as an almost perfect place "free from the harsh realities of the world outside the gates, projecting for themselves in the village a form of utopia" (Korol-Evans 2009:167). The fantasy of the renaissance festival allows it to take on a feeling of being a utopian site. And there are those within the subculture, many of whom seem reluctant to return to their more mundane occupations during the rest of the week or the off season, who would seek to make more of their lives like what they experience during the faire. "When the destructive realities of the outside world seem far greater, the faire provides a way to escape the reality of twenty-first century America" (Korol-Evans2009:167). In this way, we can think of the renaissance festival subculture as an almost utopian setting, in the sense of seeking out that "perfect" social atmosphere offered by the instasticive context of the festival itself.

The renaissance festival is a perfect example for examining in the light of Goffman's dramaturgical analysis. For all those working and performing at the faire, but especially the street cast, whose role it is to construct the fantasy for all to share in by way of their interactions with both one another and with visitors, this is especially true. Their performances are fully interactive and almost completely improvised constructs which enable the context to take on enough life for participants, patrons and performers alike, to suspend enough of their disbelief—to escape the mundane world—and experience that shared fantasy. Simply donning costumes, although a strong visual component of the transformation, is not enough for cast members to shift from their regular identities to their faire characters. There are also many other dramaturgical elements involved such as props, scripts in the form of language or accent, changes in body movements, and even the setting itself, which are all essential parts of their performance, both as individual characters and as a group portraying the inhabitants of the village or kingdom. If at any moment any of these were to be ignored or left to chance, the magic might be broken and the fantasy state ended.

At the same time, the frontstage-backstage dynamic plays out with the fantasy of romantic history in the frontstage, and all other aspects of the 21st century as the backstage, whether they add to the fantasy itself or not.

The weeks of cast rehearsals, costuming workshops, and jousting practice that happen in preparation for the faire itself are a large part of this. But so are the long car rides, cell phone calls, and credit card transactions which take place in the peripheries of the festival that also facilitate the overall experience.

Nerd Culture: Fantasy, Stigma, and Identity

There appears to be a certain degree of pride among rennies concerning their classification as "nerds," or "weirdos," or any other less-than-complimentary label that might be applied to those who take near-obsessive delight in certain hobbies or fandoms in fantasy, fiction-based, or romanticized realms. In cases of intentional non-conformity social strain still occurs. In fact the refusal to conform may itself be a reaction to minor social sanctioning by the normative group. While it has been theorized that individuals learn to be deviant by association with other deviants, motivation for non-conformity has a social character, even if much of the activity itself is carried on in a solitary fashion (Becker 1963), such as one's choices involving fandom, as appears to be a contributing factor toward involvement in the renaissance festival subculture. Sometimes consumption of popular media may take the place of face-to-face interaction as a means of inducting the individual into the subculture. Each subculture then has its own ideology which is tied to the group's collective identity (Becker 2003), and rennies are no exception. They simply wear their differences, quite literally in terms of costumes, for everyone to see.

Renfaire participants spoke about the reactions they received from family members ranging from "I don't get it," or "When are you going to grow up?" to one playtron whose ex-husband had gone so far as to confiscate her garb and refuse to let her attend faire because he was so embarrassed by how she preferred to spend her weekends. The stereotype of "D&D (Dungeons & Dragons) geeks, or renfaire geeks, or any other kind of geeks," as Phillip McGuinness put it, carries with it a level of stigma. Our culture is full of rumors of the 30-something, underemployed science fiction fan or fantasy gamer who lives in his parents' basement, munching cheese puffs and swilling soda while rarely venturing forth except to pick up the latest issue of his multiple comic book subscriptions. While this stereotype did not appear to hold true for those individuals I spoke with, at least not all the components of it at once in the same individual, the stigma of being a "nerd" or "geek" still exists. Lady Sersha spoke about the challenges of learning to interact with patrons as a member of the street cast "to someone who grew up as a wallflower." "All the people who didn't quite fit into regular society, this is their playground," comedic musician Iris said. "Because this is the place where the misfit toys are all welcome," her sister and performing partner Rose added.

And it is not simply the stigma of being a geek or nerd that rennies encounter. To the more "normal" members of the surrounding communities where renaissance festivals take place for several weekends each year, festival workers may be viewed as ne'er-do-well vagrants, threatening to disturb order of the outer community, socially if not in any criminal sense. "This threat derives from identity perceptions of the actors and other people working the festival as employing certain 'types of people'—people who appear, to them, to live outside the bounds of normal society" (Gunnels 2004:226). The faire may be thought of as attracting a "deviant" segment of the population (Gunnels 2009). "Some places you go the townies see rennies as gypsies, carnies, wild hippies who might bring trouble," said Jacob, the proprietor of a traveling shop who spends nine months of every year on the road working at renfaires, following a circuit of venues in order to sell his wares. However, I did not personally witness anything that would make me think there was any substance to this bad reputation of the "road rennies," as they are called, the boothies and performers who travel the faire circuit.

It should also be noted that in the part of the country where I did my field investigation—the Ohio Valley region of the Midwest—the general culture is markedly conservative and religious, with less tolerance for social differences than in more cosmopolitan areas.

> "There's nothing that goes on at faire that is negative or should be seen as negative, and it's not something to be shunned because of it being a fantasy type atmosphere. Some people have trouble understanding. For a time people thought the faire was an evil place," said the man portraying King Robert the Bruce.

My observations did not find the alleged rumors of sinister happenings to be true. In fact, it was pointed out to me that "rennies believe in honor," as Lee Bishop said. They are incredibly supportive of one another, pooling resources whenever someone around them at the faire is in need. I even experienced this myself one evening when the battery in my car had died and I needed a jump. Three men and one woman, only two of whom seemed to know each other and none of whom knew me, all volunteered their time, vehicles, and jumper cables to assist me. They believe that "chivalry never really died," as Crystiana put it. "It's just hiding out here at the renfaire." They are the kind of people who are more likely to help with neighborhood clean-ups than to pillage the local town, such as the Commodore's pirates who, as he explained, take on a yearly charity project such as raising funds for breast cancer research or the RESCU Foundation which helps uninsured rennies pay medical bills. And many festival employees are in fact residents of surrounding communities or theatre students from nearby universities (KorolEvans 2010).

According to strain theory in the study of deviant behavior, "people are more likely to pursue illegitimate means of attaining culturally prescribed goals when they are blocked from accessing the institutionalized means to those goals" (Featherstone and Deflem 2003:472). The strain of not being able to achieve normative objectives set forth by the parent culture, whether financial or social, can lead to various adaptations, including innovation and retreatism. While traditional strain theory describes retreatism as a retreat from social interactions and the normative goals of a society, sometimes to the point of dropping out of society, what I see among renaissance festival participants is a retreat to subculture; in this case that of the renaissance festival. And while it may seem at first that this is retreatism, the temporary nature of renaissance festivals themselves, that participants only attend on weekends for a few weeks worth of a season in any one locale and then return to their regular lives the rest of the time, makes this more of an innovation. The social bonds and friendships involved in this retreat into the renfaire subculture are in fact a pro-social innovative adaptation to the negative emotions associated with feelings of outsiderdom or the stigma associated with "nerdy" interests.

Strain theory is based largely on the concept of anomie resulting from experiencing blocked access to legitimized means to achieve culturally determined goals (Featherstone and Deflem 2003). However individuals may still encounter the frustration and other negative emotions that can be associated with s strain theory, resulting from more personal experiences such as those involved in the stigma of having "nerdy" hobbies like the renfaire, or simply not feeling like they fit in with mainstream society or the expectations of their daily lives. Instead of looking at the means and goals as economic success, but rather seeing them as "social success," as the ability and ambition to build social status and/or capital rather than just money, the picture becomes clearer. In short, the inability to "fit in" socially, or of feeling like one is already outside of the normative culture often through feelings of identifying with or as part of a deviant subculture, can create the same strain experienced in more conventional contexts of anomie. The culturally-induced pressure to conform thus the turn to other, subcultural, settings with alternate norms and goals which do not induce such pressure or in which the culture's ideals and norms are a better fit or more readily attainable or acceptable to the individuals involved.

One theme prevails among renaissance faire participants, at some point in their lives nearly every one of them has experienced a feeling of not "fitting in" with mainstream culture, of being "different." It is this feeling of being different which can lead individuals to feel social strain similar to that described by Merton, Agnew, and other strain theorists. Strain, in turn, is a chief motivation toward deviant behavior (Agnew 1997). Whether rennies do in fact have many normal social connections outside the subculture, such as families and jobs, they repeatedly expressed to me their own feelings of being a social outcast or not fitting in on some level, as discussed above.

However, their retreat to the social acceptance within the subculture is an innovative adaptation to the stigma they perceive and the ensuing feelings of general social strain. The bonds they are able to form with like minded others who share their social paradigm of the renfaire's romanticized version of history offers them a pro-social context which still allows for their desired performance of alternate identity. For example, one playtron who was the mother of a 9 year old boy who was new to the cast as the king's page, talked about the positive masculine role models her son had found in the king, his knight-bodyguard, and personal squire. And Jezzie the Pirate Queen at QRF related a tale in which she was able to help boost the self-esteem of a patron who visited her shop.

> "I was working selling costumes, and a woman of probably about 70 walked in. She was looking at the gowns and said that they were so beautiful but that she didn't think she could wear any of

them. She didn't think they would fit because she's had a mastectomy and she couldn't fill out the bodice right. I told her, 'You don't understand, I work magic.' I said for her to take one of the full-length chemises into the dressing room and come out when she had it on. Then I put her into one of the gowns, one that was two sizes smaller than she might normally have worn, and I laced her up in it really tight. It made a crease for cleavage. Then I puffed out her chemise so that it looked like she had the littlest bit of cleavage under the bodice of that dress. And she stood there and looked in the mirror and started crying. She said, 'I haven't seen these in years. Thank you so much!' She bought the outfit and walked out. She was so proud she had a bosom. And I just cried because here was a woman who thought it was the end for her, and yet here she felt sexy at 70 years old."

Hoelter (1983) describes identity and self-definition as partially based on perceptions of others' appraisals and of one's own comparison of self with others, similar to Cooley's theory of the Looking Glass Self. Based on the goals set forth by mainstream culture, primarily presented in mass media, these comparisons may or may not be pleasant and could be the source of frustration and strain for those individuals who find themselves on the short end of the measuring stick, especially socially in the case of many of the outsiders who would rather pursue alternate goals than those which American media sets for them. This is certainly not the only impetus driving individuals to become involved in renaissance festivals. However, the drive to express aspects of identity which might not be readily accepted in everyday life, and be accepted for doing so, does play a part. And it is here that the individual fantasies and alternate identities interact and flow together to create the shared fantasy of the festival.

The Renaissance Festival Subculture and Retreatism

One of the initial questions posed during the early phases of this project was that of whether social strain and stigma related to the pursuit of this type of "nerdy" hobbies, or if the inability to fit in with mainstream society in a satisfactory or meaningful way might be a factor in why renaissance festival participants do what they do, with regard to both creating the shared fantasy social environment and to their creation and performance of an alternate identity. Therefore some discussion is warranted on the topic.

"Deviance is the failure to obey group rules. A person may break the rules of one group by the very act of abiding by the rules of another group" (Becker 1963:8). Deviance is in fact a constructed concept created by each social group by making rules whose infraction thus constitutes deviance. And the deviant behavior in question need not be criminal or harmful, merely something that elicits an adverse reaction by virtue of having challenged the cultural status quo. We see this evidenced in the way those individuals who may not conform to cultural norms are sometimes ostracized, called "nerd" or otherwise labeled as "uncool." Becker

(1963) uses the term "outsiders" to refer to those individuals who are judged deviant by others and thus made to stand outside the circle of "normal" group members. Thus we may see those individuals who have been harshly judged, perhaps for unconventional interests in areas of activity congruent with the renaissance festival subculture, but not with mainstream America which favors commodified consumption over nostalgic participation experiences.

Still, deviance is defined by those in the social majority. Merton termed the disjunction between society's goals and conventional means to attain them as "anomie" or strain (Featherstone 2003). And most assuredly the renaissance festival workers and other members of the subculture who regularly attend the faires in costume and portray an alternate persona do not display, at least in this context, the normative behaviors of everyday America. Popular culture and advertising media have created an environment in American society in which expectations of success may be beyond the reach of many people. Goals need not involve only the ambitions of financial success. They can also be those of acceptance, beauty, popularity, and finding a place of respect among one's peers. However, this kind of social goal may not be attainable for all, and therein lies a source of social strain which, as every unpopular person knows, can lead to necessary adaptations in both action and self-image. Individuals adjust to patterns of means and goals in one of five modes of individual adaptation: conformity, ritualism, innovation, retreatism, or rebellion. Conformity and ritualism are normative adaptations; retreatism and rebellion are deviant alternatives; innovation may or may not be seen as deviant depending on the form the innovation takes, though it is always a deviation from the existing norm (Agnew 1997). It was the possible adaptations to social strain which might lead participants to retreat to the renaissance faire subculture in search of acceptance which led me to consider this question.

This is not to say that renaissance festival participants all come from lower socioeconomic backgrounds and have turned to the subculture for innovative means of achieving success, although that does sometimes occur. However, if we examine cultural means and goals as social rather than economic, we can see how outsiders who have been socially ostracized for being different might seek this subculture as a kind of haven where they might find more meaningful interactions and a sense of belonging.

Previous sociological work exists on how social strain and feelings of outsiderdom can lead to various adaptations, not the least of which is retreatism (Agnew 1997, Becker 1963). Much of this work deals with deviance as relates to criminal or delinquent behavior, problematic to society as a whole. I would argue that in the case of renaissance festivals, that retreatism as a temporary adaptation to strain may certainly be non-normative—thus deviant by the most basic of definitions—it is not a form of deviance which is in its essence detrimental to either society or the participants involved. A couple thousand geeks getting together with others of like mind, dressing up in funny clothes, and speaking to one another in a poor imitation of an Elizabethan dialect would seem weird to anyone outside of this context. But the sense of having found one's place—one's tribe as it were—and acting according to the norms of that subculture is not so different in sociological terms from the fanatical behavior of sports fans on the day of a big game.

Challenges of Studying this Subculture

The study of the renaissance festival subculture presents many challenges, foremost that scholarship on renaissance faires themselves is somewhat limited. While recent studies do exist in the areas of theatre studies as well as recreation and tourism science, very little, if any, work has been undertaken from a sociological standpoint. Secondly, participation in renaissance festivals is, for the most part, seasonal and migratory. Each festival takes place during four to eight weekends once a year, with some rennies traveling on to the next faire in a circuit, but most simply returning to jobs and lives in their local communities. Any attempt at census type demographical study will prove difficult except in projecting how a sample might reflect the whole.

Not only are many members of this subculture transitory, most notably boothies and stage performers who may travel much of the year following the faire season circuit for work, but level of involvement greatly from one individual to another, in the various festivals and subculture itself. Some participants actively take part in the faires, but only occasionally. Others have rearranged their entire way of life around the ideals the subculture espouses. This seems to have a relationship to the levels of intrasticivity Korol-Evans (2009) describes regarding patrons' participation in interaction with the fantasy realm created inside the renaissance faire. Based on my observations, one of the reasons for the varying degree of immersion into the subculture is one of social bonds. With all the references to their renfaire friends as "family" from so many of the participants in various roles within the festival itself, performers and playtrons alike, it appears that the more acceptance and communitas each individual feels as part of the group or subculture, the more they will be willing to invest of their time and resources in order to be involved. And while this specific question of the relationship between level of immersion and social bonds was not fully addressed in this study, it would be interesting to seek an answer to in the future.

Conclusion

Whether through an interest in history, fandom of medieval adventures in popular media, or some other similar activity such as RPGs or online gaming, renaissance festival participants collectively construct the social context in both their interactions and the physical manifestation of the festival grounds in order to share in a collective fantasy. They seek to spend time with like minded people who enjoy the same activities and share a similar romanticized view of that time in history. They create alternate identities, called personas, dress in fanciful costumes of the time period, and even call each other by different names in order to help bring their inner ideals to life in their interactive performances.

Because this activity—a hobby to some but an immersive subculture to others— can be seen as a frivolous, perhaps somewhat "nerdy" attempt to escape the responsibilities of adult life in mainstream society, there is some stigma involved in taking part in renaissance faires. Conversely, some renfaire enthusiasts have felt themselves to be outsiders, perhaps because of their interests in similarly stigmatized things, whether science fiction or fantasy media, games, or other interests that those around them who prefer more normative interests such as sports or celebrity gossip show disdain toward. In either case, the strains of being an outsider lead rennies to band together within their subculture as a retreat to a social context where they become part of their own unique in-group. "This is like the island of misfit toys," was how one woman put it, herself a twenty-year renaissance faire veteran. This kind of fantasy subculture is a pro-social innovative adaptation to perceived stigma and the resulting feelings of social strain.

Because participation takes on such strong meaning in the lives of many participants, specifically the performers, workers, and playtrons, if not the plain clothes tourist-type patrons, taking part in these events and becoming part of the subculture can affect their lives outside the festival itself. Sometimes financial decisions are made giving preference to renfaire activities and related purchases. And certainly relationships of all kinds are formed throughout the process. For some individuals, life inside the faire can seem more real, or the experiences more authentic with meaning than life in what rennies term the mundane world. And their formation and performance of alternate identities reflects this.

Both the playtrons attending the festival and the performers and boothies working there create an alternate identity—a persona or character—which they then behave as, to varying degrees, in their interactions with others at the faire and in the subculture. In this study I found that an individual's role in the festival context, either performer or playtron, has a bearing on whether the collective fantasy setting itself or the personal fantasy is more of an influence on the creation and performance of this alternative identity. For those working at the renfaire, whether they are street cast, stage performer, or someone working in one of the shops, the collective fantasy drives their performance of identity. They have a specific role in the fantasy context of the "village" which is very much part of the overall structure of creating the tangible manifestation of the festival itself, therefore the theme of the faire and the scenario it is meant to convey determines how their persona is performed to some degree. In fact some street cast members take on the character of actual historical figures or other historically plausible villagers as assigned to them by directors or other festival officials. The performers then bring life to the persona by adding their own personality to the "mask" of the character. But for playtrons, who pay to get through the gates and attend the renaissance festival in costume and play along with the interactive fantasy at the faire, create and perform their alternate identities with complete freedom of choice. Several factors may influence each individual, including popular media in the form of books or films, the influences of friends who already have established personas, or even their own imaginings of how their life might have been like had they been born into this romanticized historical setting. As the Commodore said, "I really am a pirate!" And it will be quite fascinating in the future to examine what social forces are at work which influence the degree of salience of these alternate identities.

For Further Study

It has not been within the scope of this paper to delve into all possible applications of identity and subculture theory as might be applicable to the renaissance festival subculture. The issue of values, gender norms, and sexual practices alone is one such question which future scholars might seek to address. The possibility exists for further study in examining subcultures with regard to anomie and strain, particularly those which are based in the taste cultures which manifest out of mass media's play toward niche markets. There were also several questions that arose during the course of this project which could be studied in greater depth than I was able to examine here. For instance, how might popular culture factors be involved in the creation of alternative or non-normative identities expressed in the festival setting? And how does the renaissance festival create a safe zone for the expression of non-normative identity within this subculture?

The renaissance festival context, and the larger overarching "geek" subculture, of which renfaires are only one facet, is a social environment rich with information about persona building process and embodiment of alternative identity, as well as that of the carnivalesque setting and the communitas that arises from the shared experiences thereof. One stage performer and life-long rennie, who performs under the name Doktor Kaboom, suggested that for further study I should get a job at a renaissance festival, staying on site through the week and really integrating into the subculture for a longer period of time to get a more in-depth insider's view of social processes as they occur away from any audience of visitors.

It would also be interesting to do more precise work on the development of non-normative alternative identity, as can be found in many settings such as comic book and science fiction conventions, MMORPGs (Nardi 2010, Gilsdorf 2009), role playing games (McGonigal 2011, Bowman 2010), and other festival settings. I also noticed emergent themes of femininity embodiment that speak of a blending of traditional gender roles and third wave feminism within this subculture. Considering the number of women who dress provocatively and self-identify as "wenches," it would be interesting to further build upon this study and make an inquiry into the use of femininity as cultural capital in the geek subculture.

Studies of deviance have pointed to retreatism into "utopian" subculture as an adaptation which allows for more authentic identity expression. By examining the renaissance festival subculture through the lens of strain and subculture theories we can see how the collective identities formed within the renaissance festival subculture, the innovative means of expression, and even entrepreneurialism and purchasing choices involved in the business ventures inside the subculture itself show it to be its own constructed insular society. Social strain combined with the influence of popular media work to drive participants toward retreatism in the subculture as a social setting in which they can find meaningful interaction with others who share their social paradigm and romanticized version of history. Understanding of the urge to withdraw from mainstream society in favor of liminal subcultures, in the quest for meaningful relationships and recreational interaction such as can be found at renaissance festivals, promises to be of growing interest to sociologists.

For one thing is certain, as mundane life becomes less satisfactory, such as in times of economic downturn, the desire to escape—to retreat into an interactive, participatory fantasy realm—only stands to remain or increase. Since their inception in the 1960s, renaissance festivals have continued to grow and spread across the United States as a form of weekend entertainment for some, and as a subculture and social network for others. And through the study of the forms of play people chose to take part in, we can learn more about our own culture.

References

Agnew, Robert. 1997. "The Nature and Determinants of Strain: Another Look at Durkheim and Merton." Pp. 27-51 in The Future of Anomie Theory, edited by N. Passas and R. Agnew. Boston, MA: Northeastern University Press.

Bakhtin, Mikhail. 1968. Rabelais and His World. Bloomington, IN: Indiana University Press.

Becker, Howard S. 1963. Outsiders: Studies in the Sociology of Deviance. The Free Press, New York.

Benford, Robert D. and David A. Snow. 2000. "Framing Processes and Social Movements: An Overview and Assessment. Annual Review of Sociology 26:611- 639.

Berger, Peter and Thomas Luckmann. 1966. The Social Construction of Reality. New York: Anchor Books.

Bowman, Sarah L. 2010. The Functions of Role-Playing Games: How Participants Create Community, Solve Problems, and Explore Identity. Jefferson, NC: McFarland & Company, Inc.

Bucholtz, Mary. 2002. "Youth and Cultural Practice."

Annual Review of Anthropology 31:525-552.

Campbell, Joseph. 1988. The Power of Myth. New York, NY: Anchor Books.

Cohen, A. P. 1985. The Symbolic Construction of Community. New York: Routledge.

Cramer, Michael. 2010. Medieval Fantasy as Performance. Lanham, MD: The Scarecrow Press, Inc.

Featherstone, Richard and Mathieu Deflem. 2003. "Anomie and Strain: Context and Consequences of Merton's Two Theories." Sociological Inquiry 73(4):471-489.

Fine, Gary A. 1983. Shared Fantasy: Role-Playing Games as Social Worlds. Chicago, IL: University of Chicago Press.

Gilsdorf, Ethan. 2009. Fantasy Freaks and Gaming Geeks: An Epic Quest for Reality Among Role Players, Online Gamers, and Other Dwellers of Imaginary Realms. Guilford, CT: The Lyons Press.

Goffman, Erving. 1959. The Presentation of Self in Everyday Life. New York: Anchor Books.

Goulding, Christina and Michael Saren. 2009. "Performing Identity: an Analysis of Gender Expressions at the Whitby Goth Festival." Consumption Markets & Culture 12(1):27-46.

Gunnels, Jennifer S. 2004. "Let the Car Burn, We're Going to the Faire: History, Performance, Community and Identity within the Renaissance Festival." PhD dissertation, The University of Texas at Austin.

Hoelter, Jon W. 1983. "The Effects of Role Evaluation and Commitment on Identity Salience." Social Psychology Quarterly 46(2):140-147.

Huizinga, Johan. 1950. Homo Ludens: A Study of the

Play-Element in Culture. Boston, MA: Beacon Press.

Jancovich, Mark. 2002. "Cult Fictions: Cult Movies, Subcultural Capital and the Production of Cultural Distinctions. Cultural Studies 16(2):306-322.

Kim, Hyounggon. 2004. "Serious Leisure, Participation and Experience in Tourism: Authenticity and Ritual in a Renaissance Festival." PhD dissertation, Department of Recreation, Park, and Tourism Sciences, Texas A&M University, College Station, TX.

Korol-Evans, Kimberly T. 2009. Renaissance Festivals: Merrying the Past and Present. Jefferson, NC: McFarland & Company, Inc.

Lancaster, Kurt. 1999. Warlocks and Warpdrive: Contemporary Fantasy Entertainments with Interactive and Virtual Environments. Jefferson, NC: McFarland & Company, Inc.

McGonigal, Jane. 2011. Reality Is Broken: Why Games Make Us Better and How They Can Change the World. New York: Penguin Press.

Nardi, Bonnie A. 2010. My Life as A Night Elf Priest: An Anthropological Account of World of Warcraft. Ann Arbor, MI: University of Michigan Press.

O'Donnell, Patrick. 2004. The Knights Next Door: Everyday People Living Middle Ages Dreams. New York: iUniverse, Inc.

Pearson, Roberta. 2007. "Bachies, Bardies, Trekkies, and Sherlockians." Fandom: Identities and Communities in a Mediated World. New York: New York University Press.

Rojek, Chris. 2005. "An Outline of the Action Approach to Leisure Studies." Leisure Studies 24(1):13-25.

Stahl, Geoff. 1999. "Still 'Winning Space?': Updating

Subcultural Theory." In-visible Culture. March 10, 2010. http://rochester.edu

Weitzer, Ronald. 2007. "Prostitution as a Form of Work." Sociology Compass 1(1):143- 155.

Williams, J. Patrick, Sean Q. Hendricks, and W. Keith Winkler, Editors. 2006. Gaming as Culture: Essays on Reality, Identity and Experience in Fantasy Games. Jefferson, NC: McFarland & Company, Inc. Thesis and Dissertation Services

About the Author

Heather E. Dumas holds a master's degree in sociology from Ohio University, and has taught at four universities in Ohio and Kentucky.

Writing under the name *Heather Ember Amsden*, she is the author of the cozy urban fantasy Evergreen Witches series, and the medieval fantasy Everwood series. She lives near Lexington, Kentucky with her two cats, Bruce and Luna, who enjoy interrupting the creative process. On any given weekend you're likely to find her at a renaissance faire when she's not writing, sewing, or working on her handspun yarn business - a real life woolmonger. She's also a sociology professor, a master seamstress, and historical costume designer. Likes: cats, coffee, and cable knit sweaters. Dislikes: stink bugs, seafood, and wet socks.

You can find updates about Heather's books on social media.
Instagram: @evergreenwitches
Facebook: @Evergreen Witches

www.ingramcontent.com/pod-product-compliance
Lightning Source LLC
Chambersburg PA
CBHW050818250726

48653CB00006B/2289